Egyptian Cookbook

Enjoy Authentic Egyptian Cooking with 50 Delicious Egyptian Recipes

By
BookSumo Press
All rights reserved

Published by
http://www.booksumo.com

ENJOY THE RECIPES?

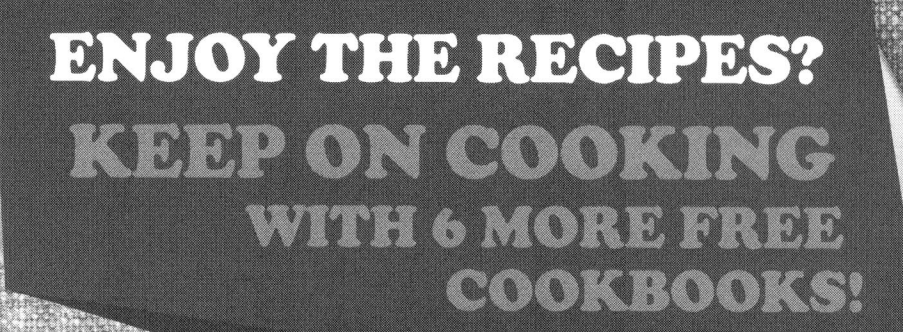

KEEP ON COOKING WITH 6 MORE FREE COOKBOOKS!

Visit our website and simply enter your email address to join the club and receive your 6 cookbooks.

http://booksumo.com/magnet

https://www.instagram.com/booksumopress/

https://www.facebook.com/booksumo/

LEGAL NOTES

All Rights Reserved. No Part Of This Book May Be Reproduced Or Transmitted In Any Form Or By Any Means. Photocopying, Posting Online, And / Or Digital Copying Is Strictly Prohibited Unless Written Permission Is Granted By The Book's Publishing Company. Limited Use Of The Book's Text Is Permitted For Use In Reviews Written For The Public.

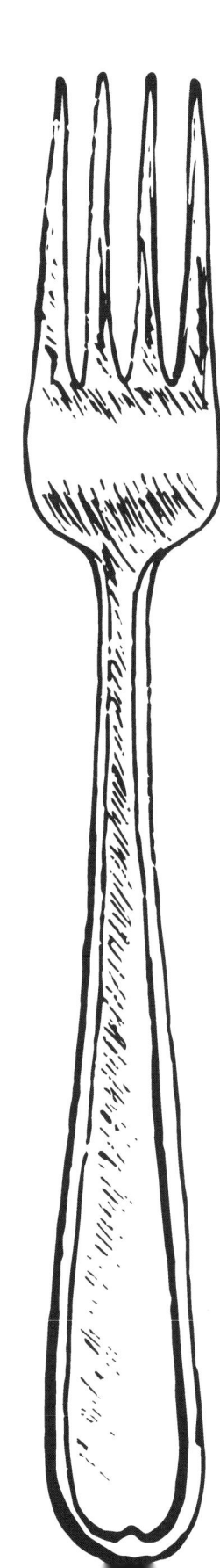

Table of Contents

Fasulya Beeda Barda 7

Tabilch 8

Sambousak Bi Lahm 9

Fahmi's Famous Koshari 10

Charoset 11

Pan Braised Chicken 12

Bastirma 13

Spiced Seafood Kofta 14

Gebna Makleyah 15

Lemon Chicken Casserole 16

Spinach Omelet 17

Egyptian Pot Pies 18

Chickpea and Cabbage Stew 19

Saniyit Kofta 20

Seafood Dolmas 21

Kar Assaly 22

Fatta (Lamb Soup) 23

Taagiin Saamaak 24

Ful Nabed 25

How to Make Lamb Chops 26

Basturma and Sujuq 27

Beef Patties with White Sauce 28

Masa'a 29

Molokheya 30

Skakshuka 31

Fish Kabobs 32

Chicken Soup Arabiya 33

How to Make Falafels 34

Cairo Street Grilled Chicken 35

5-Ingredient Egyptian Rice 36

Mashed Carrots 37

Stuffed Mushroom 38

How to Make Fava Beans 39

Chocolate Cake 40

Onion and Cucumber Salad 41

Mihallabiya 42

Eggah 43

Stuffed Grape Leaves: (Dolmas) 44

Koras 45

Alexandria Chocolate Cake 46

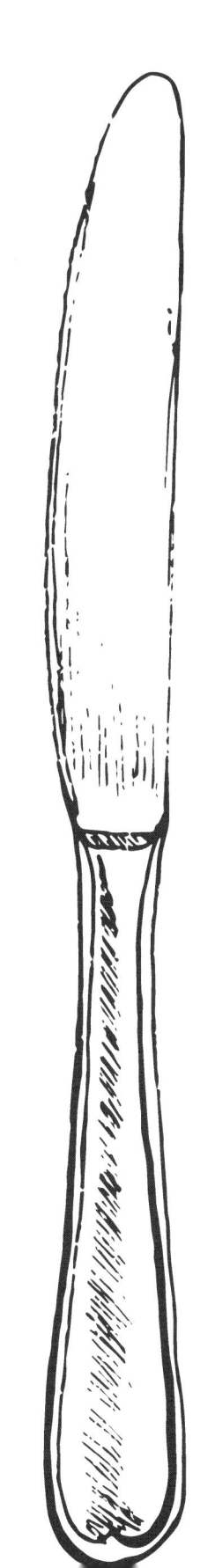

Ful Mudammes 47

Omm 'Ali 48

Lentil Hot Pot 49

Bangar Bil Zabadi 50

Kosa Matbukha Bi l Zabadi 51

Alternative Koshari 52

Dukka (Egyptian Spice Blend) 53

Raspberry and Peach Fruit Cups 54

Rice Pudding 55

Cauliflower: (قرنبيط) 56

Feta Omelet: (عجة الجبن) 57

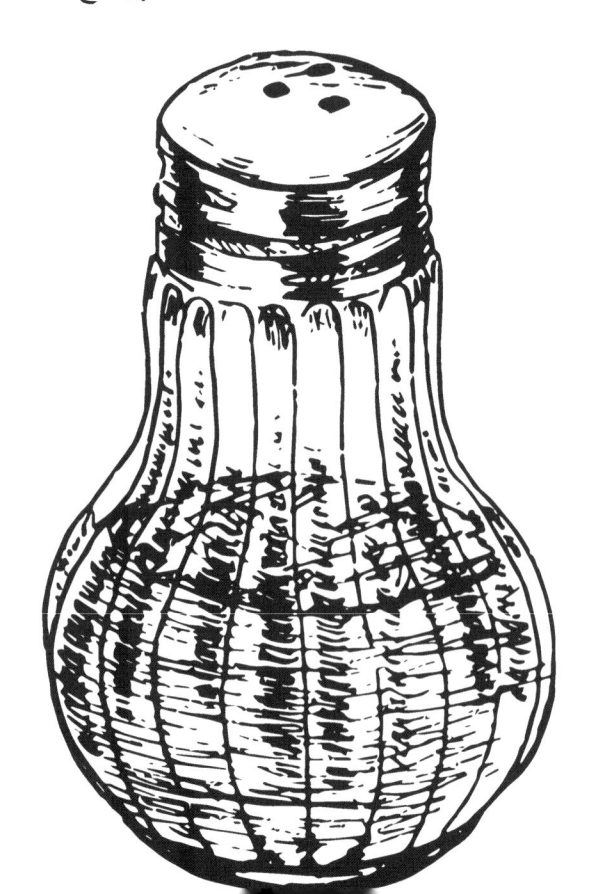

Fasulya Beeda Barda (Bean Salad)

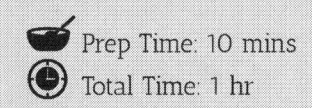

Prep Time: 10 mins
Total Time: 1 hr

Servings per Recipe: 6
Calories   80.1
Fat   2.6g
Cholesterol   0.0mg
Sodium   80.3mg
Carbohydrates   11.6g
Protein   3.3g

Ingredients

- 1 C. navy beans
- 1 small red onion
- 1 C. parsley
- 2 tomatoes
- 1 tbsp olive oil
- 1 tbsp vinegar
- 1 tbsp lemon juice
- salt, to taste
- pepper, to taste
- 1 garlic clove
- 1/4 tsp cumin
- 1 dash cayenne

Directions

1. Place the beans in a large bowl and cover it with water. Let it soak for an overnight.
2. Place a large pot over medium heat. Add to it the drain bean and cover it with water and some sat. Put on the lid and cook it for 45 min to 1 h or until it is soft.
3. Remove the beans from the water. Place it in a colander to drain. Discard the tomato seeds and chop them. Cut the onion into thin slices. Finely chop the parsley.
4. Get a small bowl: Whisk in it the olive oil, vinegar, lemon juice, salt and pepper, cumin and cayenne to make the dressing.
5. Get a large mixing bowl: Toss in it the beans with tomato, onion, parsley and the dressing. Serve it with some flat bread.
6. Enjoy.

TABILCH
(Zucchini Stew with Rice)

Prep Time: 5 mins
Total Time: 25 mins

Servings per Recipe: 6
Calories   274.4
Fat   2.2g
Cholesterol   0.1mg
Sodium   760.6mg
Carbohydrates   57.8g
Protein   7.1g

Ingredients

1 medium zucchini
2 C. canned green beans
2 C. tomato sauce
curry, to taste
sage, to taste
tarragon, to taste

1 tbsp lemon zest
1/3 onion
4 C. water
2 C. brown rice
2 beef bouillon cubes

Directions

1. Prepare the rice according to the instructions on the package. Stir in the bouillon cubes to it when it starts boiling.
2. Stir the zucchini, green beans and onion in tomato sauce in a large pan. Lower the heat and cook them for 12 min over medium heat. Stir in the spices and cook them for 8 min.
3. Serve your zucchini over the brown rice warm.
4. Enjoy.

Sambousak Bi Lahm (Lamb Pies)

🥣 Prep Time: 30 mins
⏱ Total Time: 1 hr

Servings per Recipe: 1
Calories   361.6
Fat   24.1g
Cholesterol   27.5mg
Sodium   120.7mg
Carbohydrates   25.8g
Protein   10.1g

Ingredients

Pastry:
- 2/3 C. oil
- 2/3 C. warm water
- 1/2 tsp salt
- 3 C. flour

Filling:
- 1 large onion, finely chopped
- 1 lb ground lamb or 1 lb ground beef
- 1/2 tsp allspice
- 2/3 tsp cinnamon
- salt and pepper, to taste
- 1/4 C. water
- 6 tbsp pine nuts, toasted

Topping:
- 1 egg yolk, for the glaze
- sesame seeds

Directions

1. Before you do anything preheat the oven to 350 F.
2. To make the dough:
3. Get a large mixing bowl: Combine in it the oil, water and salt. Stir them well. Add the flour gradually while mixing until you get a smooth dough.
4. Cover the dough with a kitchen towel and place it aside to rest for 1 h.
5. To make the filling:
6. Place a large pan over medium heat. Cook in it the lamb for 8 min while breaking it. Stir in the onion and cook them for 3 min.
7. Stir in some salt, pepper, allspice and cinnamon with water to deglaze the pan. Cook them for 6 min. Fold in the pine nuts and remove the mix from the heat.
8. Divide the dough into 12 or 20 pieces. Roll each piece of dough into circle until it becomes 1/4 inch thick on a floured surface.
9. Place 2 tsp of the filling on the center of 1 dough circle if you are making 20 dumplings and 3 tbsp of filling if you are making 12 large dumpling.
10. Fold the free side for the filling to make half a circle. Press the side with a fork to seal the edges. Place them over a greased baking sheet.
11. Get a small mixing bowl: Whisk in it 1 tsp of water with the egg yolk. Brush the dumplings with the mix. Cook them in the oven for 32 min.
12. Allow the dumplings to lose heat for few minutes then serve it warm.
13. Enjoy.

FAHMI'S FAMOUS
Koshari

Prep Time: 15 mins
Total Time: 1 hr 15 mins

Servings per Recipe: 10
Calories	436.3
Fat	7.9g
Cholesterol	0.0mg
Sodium	476.5mg
Carbohydrates	76.4g
Protein	13.3g

Ingredients

1 tbsp vegetable oil
1 yellow onion, finely diced
1 1/2 tsp salt
1 tsp ground cumin
1/4 tsp black pepper
1 C. black lentils or 1 C. brown lentils, washed
2 1/2 C. water
2 C. calrose rice, rinsed
3 C. water
diced tomato, 28 oz can
1 C. water
1/4 C. olive oil
1/4 C. white vinegar
2 tbsp garlic, minced
1/2 tsp ground cumin
1/2 tsp salt
1/4 tsp pure chile powder
1/4 tsp black pepper
4 C. macaroni
fried onions, to taste

Directions

1. Place a large pot over medium heat. Heat the oil in it. Sauté in it the onion for 6 min. Add the cumin with a pinch of salt and pepper. Cook them for 2 min.
2. Stir in the lentils with 2 1/2 C. of water. Cook over medium heat until they start boiling. Lower the heat to medium heat. Keep boiling it for 16 min.
3. Stir in the rice with 3 C. of water. Cook them until they start boiling. Lower the heat to low and put on the lid. Cook them for 15 min or until the rice and lentils are done.
4. Let them rest for 6 min. Remove the lid and fluff them with a fork.
5. Place a large saucepan over medium heat. Stir in it the tomatoes, water, oil, vinegar, garlic, cumin, salt, chili and pepper. Cook them over high heat until they start boiling.
6. Lower the heat and cook them for 16 min until they become thick to make the tomato sauce.
7. Cook the macaroni according to the directions on the package. Spoon some of the rice and lentils on a serving plate. Top it with some macaroni and tomato sauce.
8. Serve it warm with a dash of hot sauce to taste.
9. Enjoy.

Cairo
Charoset (Fruit Paste)

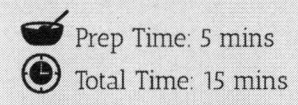

Prep Time: 5 mins
Total Time: 15 mins

Servings per Recipe: 1
Calories	934.1
Fat	19.2g
Cholesterol	0.0mg
Sodium	136.4mg
Carbohydrates	187.8g
Protein	14.4g

Ingredients

- 8 oz pitted dates, chopped
- 8 oz golden raisins
- 1/2 C. sweet red wine or apple juice
- 1/2 C. almonds, coarsely chopped

Directions

1. Stir the wine with dates and raisins in a heavy saucepan. Add enough water to cover them.
2. Cook them until the dates become soft and thicken while stirring often.
3. Spoon the mix into a serving plate and top it with the chopped almonds. Serve it.
4. Enjoy.

PAN BRAISED
Chicken

Prep Time: 45 mins
Total Time: 1 hr 45 mins

Servings per Recipe: 8
Calories	436.8
Fat	36.3g
Cholesterol	191.5mg
Sodium	109.9mg
Carbohydrates	2.8g
Protein	24.5g

Ingredients

- 8 pieces chicken
- salt
- fresh ground black pepper
- 4 garlic cloves, pressed
- 1 tsp saffron
- 1/2 C. olive oil
- 1 tbsp parsley, finely chopped
- 1 1/4 C. boiling water or 1 1/4 C. chicken stock
- 1/2 C. whole almond, blanched
- 5 hard-boiled eggs, shelled and quartered

Directions

1. Season the chicken pieces with some salt and pepper.
2. Place a large pan over medium heat. Heat the oil in it. Add the garlic with almonds. Cook them for 2 min. Stir in the saffron and cook them for 30 sec.
3. Stir in the chicken and cook it for 4 min on each side. Add the parsley with water. Put on the lid and cook them for 1 h 10 min.
4. Adjust the seasoning your chicken casserole then serve it warm.
5. Enjoy.

Bastirma
Eggs and Pastrami (Egyptian Breakfast)

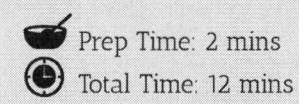

Prep Time: 2 mins
Total Time: 12 mins

Servings per Recipe: 4
Calories   119.4
Fat   6.8g
Cholesterol   232.9mg
Sodium   348.7mg
Carbohydrates   0.3g
Protein   13.1g

Ingredients

4 1/2 oz pastrami
4 -6 eggs
Pam cooking spray
salt & pepper

Directions

1. Place a pan over medium heat. Heat the oil in it. Add the pastrami and cook it for half a minute for each side. Don't overcook it.
2. Stir in the eggs with a pinch of salt and pepper. Cook them until the eggs set. Serve it warm.
3. Enjoy.

SPICED SEAFOOD
Kofta

Prep Time: 30 mins
Total Time: 1 hr

Servings per Recipe: 2
Calories 2502.7
Fat 230.3g
Cholesterol 269.2mg
Sodium 1576.8mg
Carbohydrates 64.6g
Protein 49.0g

Ingredients

275 g boneless white fish
250 g potatoes
1 garlic clove
1/2 small chopped onion
2 tbsp fresh coriander
1 tbsp flat leaf parsley
1 tsp cumin

1/2 tsp cinnamon
1/2 tsp salt
1/4 tsp pepper
2 beaten eggs
1 C. coarse fresh breadcrumb
2 C. oil

Directions

1. Bring a salted pot of water to a boil. Cook in it the fish for 12 min. Drain it. Shred it.
2. Bring another salted pot of water to a boil. Remove the potato skin and cut it into quarters. Add it to the pot and cook it for 16 min. Drain it.
3. Get a large mixing bowl: Add the potato and mash it with a fork. Combine in the coriander and parsley, crushed garlic, chopped onions, salt, pepper, cinnamon, and cumin. Mix them well.
4. Combine in the fish and mix them again while mashing the fish with a fork. Adjust the seasoning of the mix.
5. Place a large skillet over medium heat. Heat the oil in it.
6. Shape the mix into bite size pieces. Cook them in the hot skillet until they become golden brown on both sides. Serve them warm with some lemon juice.
7. Enjoy.

Asma's Gebna Makleyah (Fried Cheese)

Prep Time: 10 mins
Total Time: 20 mins

Servings per Recipe: 4
Calories 183.6
Fat 15.9g
Cholesterol 79.8mg
Sodium 436.4mg
Carbohydrates 3.1g
Protein 7.1g

Ingredients

1 C. feta cheese, crumbled
1 tbsp flour
1 egg
salt & freshly ground black pepper, to taste
2 tbsp olive oil
lemon wedge
pita bread, cut into triangles (optional, for serving)

Directions

1. Before you do anything preheat the oven to 400 F.
2. Get a large mixing bowl: Mix in it the cheese, flour, egg, salt, and pepper. Mix them well. Shape the mix into 1 inches balls.
3. Spread the oil in a baking sheet. Place the cheese bites on it and flip the coat them with oil. Cook them in the oven for 6 min.
4. Flip the cheese bites and cook them for another 6 min. Serve them warm.
5. Enjoy.

LEMON CHICKEN
Casserole

Prep Time: 10 mins
Total Time: 50 mins

Servings per Recipe: 4
Calories 279.9
Fat 4.5g
Cholesterol 85.9mg
Sodium 390.8mg
Carbohydrates 43.3g
Protein 22.2g

Ingredients

- 6 -8 boneless skinless chicken thighs
- 2 lemons
- 1/4 C. brown sugar
- 2 oz white wine vinegar
- 2 oz water
- 3/4 lb dried fig
- 1/2 tsp sea salt
- 2 tsp thyme
- 1 tbsp fresh cilantro, chopped

Directions

1. Before you do anything preheat the oven to 400 F. Grease a casserole dish.
2. Get a small mixing bowl: Whisk in it the juice of 1 lemon with brown sugar, vinegar and water. Place it aside.
3. Cut the remaining lemon in slices. Spread them in the casserole dish and top them with the figs. Top them with the chicken thighs.
4. Season them with some salt, thyme and pepper. Drizzle the sugar mix on top. Cook it in the oven for 42 min.
5. Serve your chicken casserole warm.
6. Enjoy.

Egyptian Breakfast Skillet (Spinach Omelet)

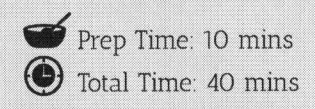

Prep Time: 10 mins
Total Time: 40 mins

Servings per Recipe: 6
Calories   273.9
Fat   15.2g
Cholesterol   186.0mg
Sodium   331.3mg
Carbohydrates   23.5g
Protein   12.1g

Ingredients

12 oz fresh Baby Spinach
2 tbsp canola oil or 2 tbsp vegetable oil
2 medium onions, chopped
2 medium tomatoes, peeled and chopped
salt
fresh ground pepper
6 eggs

1/4 tsp nutmeg
2 tbsp canola oil or 2 tbsp vegetable oil
1 (15 oz) cans chickpeas, rinsed and drained

Directions

1. Clean the spinach with some water and drain them. Bring a small saucepan of water to a boil. Stir in the spinach and put on the lid. Cook it for 5 min.
2. Drain the spinach and place it in a sieve aside.
3. Place a large pan over medium heat. Heat 2 tbsp of oil in it. Add the onion and cook it for 3 min. Stir in the tomato with a pinch of salt and pepper. Sauté them for 14 min.
4. Before you do anything preheat the oven broiler.
5. Get a mixing bowl: Whisk in it the eggs with nutmeg powder, a pinch of salt and pepper. Stir the cooked onion and tomato with spinach.
6. Place a pan over medium heat. Heat the rest of the oil in it. Add the eggs and veggies mix. Spread them in the pan and top them with the chickpeas.
7. Cook the omelet for 13 min. Cook it in the oven broiler for 2 to 4 min. Serve it warm.
8. Enjoy.

EGYPTIAN
Pot Pies

Prep Time: 30 mins
Total Time: 1 hr

Servings per Recipe: 4
Calories	573.7
Fat	17.9g
Cholesterol	188.3mg
Sodium	1237.8mg
Carbohydrates	70.6g
Protein	31.8g

Ingredients

1 lb lean ground beef
1/2 C. plain breadcrumbs
1/4 tsp allspice
1/4 tsp nutmeg
1/8 tsp black pepper
1/8 tsp cayenne pepper
1 1/2 tsp salt
2 (16 oz) cans sweet potatoes, drained
1/4 C. brown sugar
1/4 C. low-fat milk
2 eggs
1 tbsp butter, softened
1 tbsp lemon juice
1/4 tsp cinnamon
1/8 tsp garlic powder
1 tbsp onion, minced
Tabasco sauce, to taste

Directions

1. Before you do anything preheat the oven to 350 F. Grease a pie dish.
2. Get a mixing bowl: Combine in it the beef, breadcrumbs, allspice, nutmeg, pepper, cayenne, and 1 tsp of salt. Mix them well.
3. Spoon the mix to the greased dish. Place it in the fridge for 16 min.
4. Get a mixing bowl: Combine in it the sweet potato with the rest of the ingredients. Mash them and mix them well. Spread the mix over the beef layer.
5. Cook it in the oven for 52 min. Serve it warm.
6. Enjoy.

Chickpea and Cabbage Stew

Prep Time: 10 mins
Total Time: 36 mins

Servings per Recipe: 4
Calories	235.0
Fat	2.0g
Cholesterol	0.0mg
Sodium	401.0mg
Carbohydrate	49.1g
Protein	9.1g

Ingredients

1 thinly sliced onion
1/4 C. vegetable stock (or more)
3 C. thinly sliced cabbage
1 dash salt
1 large green pepper, diced or sliced
1 (28 oz) cans diced tomatoes, undrained
1 (16 oz) cans chickpeas
1/4 C. raisins or 1/4 C. currants
2 tsp ground coriander
1/2 tsp turmeric
1/4 tsp cinnamon
1 tbsp lemon juice
salt

Directions

1. Place a stew pot over medium heat. Heat in it a splash of foil.
2. Cook in it the onion for 6 min. Stir in the cabbage with salt and cook them for 6 min.
3. Add the spices with green pepper. Cook them for 1 min.
4. Add the tomatoes with raisins and chickpeas. Put on the lid and let them cook for 16 min over low heat.
5. Stir in the lemon juice. Adjust the seasoning of your stew then serve it with some couscous.
6. Enjoy.

SANIYIT KOFTA
(Kofta Burgers)

Prep Time: 15 mins
Total Time: 45 mins

Servings per Recipe: 12
Calories   198.4
Fat   12.8g
Cholesterol   57.8mg
Sodium   79.5mg
Carbohydrates   3.4g
Protein   16.4g

Ingredients

2 1/4 lbs ground beef
2 onions
2 tbsp tomato paste
1/2 tsp nutmeg or 1/2 tsp cinnamon
3 - 4 ripe tomatoes
salt & pepper

Directions

1. Peel the onion and chop them finely.
2. Get a large mixing bowl: Combine in it the chopped onion with beef, tomato paste, spices and seasonings. Spread the mix on a greased baking sheet to make a 2 inches square.
3. Slice the square into 4 pieces. Remove the tomato skin and place them over the beef squares. Cook them in the oven for 32 min. Serve them warm.
4. Enjoy.

Egyptian Seafood Dolmas

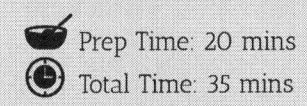

🥣 Prep Time: 20 mins
⏲ Total Time: 35 mins

Servings per Recipe: 16
Calories   202.6
Fat   16.6g
Cholesterol   55.0mg
Sodium   224.8mg
Carbohydrates   4.3g
Protein   9.1g

Ingredients

- 1 1/2 lbs skinless non oily white fish fillets, cut into 1 inch pieces
- 1 tbsp minced garlic
- 1/2 C. matzo meal
- 2 large eggs
- 1/2 tsp ground cumin
- 1 tsp kosher salt
- 1 pinch cayenne
- 1 C. vegetable oil
- 1 (8 oz) cans tomato sauce
- 1 C. water
- 2 tbsp olive oil
- 1 tbsp fresh lemon juice

Directions

1. Get a food processor: Combine in it the fish, garlic, matza meal, eggs, cumin, salt and cayenne pepper. Process them until they become smooth.
2. Place the mix in the fridge with lid on for 1 h 10 min. Shape 1/4 C. of the mix into log and flatten it a bit. Repeat the process with the rest of the mix.
3. Lay the fish logs over a lined up baking sheet.
4. Place a large pan over medium heat. Heat the oil in it. Add the fish logs and cook them in batches for 4 to 6 min on each side. Place them aside and pat them dry.
5. Place a large skillet over medium heat. Add the tomato sauce, water, olive oil, lemon juice, salt and pepper. Cook them for 4 min.
6. Stir in the rolls and cook them for 12 min over low heat. Sere your saucy fish logs warm.
7. Enjoy.

KAR ASSALY
(Autumn Pumpkin Pie)

Prep Time: 1 hr
Total Time: 3 hr

Servings per Recipe: 4
Calories 1007.0
Fat 23.8g
Cholesterol 49.4mg
Sodium 278.7mg
Carbohydrates 194.7g
Protein 14.3g

Ingredients

8 C. fresh pumpkin
3 C. sugar
2 tbsp butter
3 tbsp flour
4 C. milk
1/3 C. raisins

1/2 C. nuts

Directions

1. Peel the pumpkin and Cut them into dices.
2. Place a large pot over medium heat. Place the pumpkin in it with 1/4 C. of water and sugar. Cook them over low heat until the pumpkin becomes soft.
3. Drain the pumpkin dices and reserve the liquid in the pot. Place the pumpkin in a mixing bowl. Mash it well with a fork. Spread it in a greased casserole dish and top it with nuts and raisins.
4. Before you do anything preheat the oven to 400 F.
5. Place a heavy saucepan over medium heat. Add the butter and heat until it melts. Combine in it the flour and whisk them well. Add the milk gradually while mixing all the time.
6. Stir in the reserved pumpkin liquid. Mix them well. Cook them until they start boiling. Spread the mix all over the pumpkin nuts layer.
7. Cook the pie in the oven for 38 min. Serve it warm with some ice cream.
8. Enjoy.

Fatta
(Lamb Soup)

> 🥣 Prep Time: 15 mins
> 🕐 Total Time: 2 hr 15 mins
>
> Servings per Recipe: 8
> Calories   287.8
> Fat   18.4g
> Cholesterol   69.9mg
> Sodium   73.7mg
> Carbohydrates   16.0g
> Protein   13.6g

Ingredients

1 1/2 lbs lamb, boneless lean
2 medium onions
black pepper, freshly ground
salt, to taste
6 C. water
1 C. water
1/2 C. rice

1/4 C. ghee
2 tbsp ghee
5 garlic cloves, finely minced
1/4 C. vinegar
2 slices bread, roasted

Directions

1. Slice the lamb into dices. Place a large pot over medium heat. Pour in it 6 C. of water.
2. Add the lamb with onions, salt and pepper. Cook them until they start boiling. Lower the heat and cook the soup with the lid on for 1 h 32 min.
3. Place a large saucepan over medium heat. Stir in it the rice with 1 C. water, 1 tbsp ghee and 1/4 tsp salt. Cook them until they start boiling.
4. Put on the lid and cook them for 18 min. Remove the lamb dices from the soup and place the broth aside.
5. Place a large pan over medium heat. Heat 1 tbsp of ghee in it. Brown in it the beef dices. Place it aside. Add 1/4 C. of the ghee to the pan.
6. Cook in it the garlic for 30 sec. Turn off the heat and stir in the vinegar.
7. Stir the garlic with and broth in a large pot. Cook the soup until it starts boiling. Shred the bread and add it to soup. Serve it with the lamb and rice.
8. Enjoy.

TAAGIIN SAAMAAK
(Stewed Fish Casserole)

Prep Time: 5 mins
Total Time: 35 mins

Servings per Recipe: 4
Calories	72.2
Fat	3.6g
Cholesterol	7.6mg
Sodium	34.7mg
Carbohydrates	9.8g
Protein	1.4g

Ingredients

1 lb fish, filets
1 tbsp raisins
2 medium onions
1 C. tomatoes, canned
1/2 C. parsley, chopped
1 dash sugar
1 tbsp lemon juice
1/2 tsp cumin, ground
1 tsp pine nuts
pepper, to taste
salt, to taste
1 tbsp butter
oil, for frying

Directions

1. Before you do anything preheat the oven to 350 F.
2. Place a large pan over medium heat. Heat the oil in it. Cook in it the fish fillets until they become golden brown. Cut the onion into slices.
3. Place a large pan over medium heat. Add the butter and cook it until it melts. Add the raisins and cook them for 3 min.
4. Stir in the tomatoes, parsley and sugar. Cook them until they start boiling. Stir the cumin with lemon juice, a pinch of salt and pepper.
5. Place the fish fillets in a greased casserole dish. Pour the tomato mix all over it. Cook it in the oven for 12 min.
6. Place a small pan over medium heat. Cook in it the pine nuts until they are toasted. Sprinkle it over the fish casserole then serve it warm.
7. Enjoy.

Ful Nabed
(Fava Bean Hot Pot)

Prep Time: 15 mins
Total Time: 1 hr 5 mins

Servings per Recipe: 8
Calories   211.4
Fat   9.6g
Cholesterol   0.0mg
Sodium   6.2mg
Carbohydrates   22.8g
Protein   9.9g

Ingredients

2 C. dried fava beans
1 tsp cumin
2 garlic cloves, crushed
1/3 C. olive oil
1/4 C. lemon juice
2 tbsp fresh parsley, finely chopped
water, used to soak fava beans

Directions

1. Get a large bowl: Place in it the beans and cover them with water. Place it aside to soak for an overnight. Discard the water.
2. Place a large saucepan over medium heat. Discard the skin of the fava beans. Add it to the pan with 6 C. of water. Cook it until it starts boiling. Lower the heat and cook them for 47 min.
3. Get a food processor: Place in it the beans with the cooking water. Blend them until they become smooth.
4. Place a large saucepan over medium heat. Pour the beans mix in it. Cook it until it starts boiling. Add the cumin, garlic, lemon juice and olive oil.
5. Cook them until they start boiling again. Cook the beans mix for 6 min. Serve it warm.
6. Enjoy.

HOW TO MAKE
Lamb Chops

Prep Time: 5 mins
Total Time: 1 hr 5 mins

Servings per Recipe: 4
Calories 49.5
Fat 3.5g
Cholesterol 0.0mg
Sodium 732.1mg
Carbohydrates 4.5g
Protein 0.6g

Ingredients

2 shoulder lamb chops
1 large bunch green swiss chard, roughly chopped
4 oz tomato sauce
1/4 tsp cumin
1 tsp salt
1/4 tsp black pepper
1/4 tsp sugar
1 tbsp olive oil
1 small onion, diced finely
1 large garlic clove, minced
1/4 tsp oregano

Directions

1. Place a large pot over medium heat. Heat the oil it. Brown in it the lamb with onion for 12 min. Add the garlic and sauté them for 2 min.
2. Stir in the rest of the ingredients with 8 oz of water. Cook them until they start boiling. Put on the lid and cook them for 1 h 10 min.
3. Drain the lamb chops and shred them. Stir them back into the pot then serve it warm.
4. Enjoy.

Basturma & Sujuq (Topped Flatbread)

Prep Time: 15 mins
Total Time: 30 mins

Servings per Recipe: 16
Calories   126.9
Fat   10.2g
Cholesterol   24.7mg
Sodium   211.5mg
Carbohydrates   1.5g
Protein   7.1g

Ingredients

- 1/4 C. extra virgin olive oil
- 4 plum tomatoes, chopped
- 2 large garlic cloves, finely chopped
- 1 oz kashkaval cheese, diced
- 1 oz pastrami
- 4 links beef sausages, cut into pieces
- sea salt, and freshly ground black pepper to taste
- 16 oz mozzarella cheese, fresh chopped
- 2 tbsp finely chopped fresh flat leaf parsley

Directions

1. Before you do anything preheat the oven to its highest setting.
2. Get the pizza dough and divide it into 2 pieces. Roll the dough on a floured surface in circle shapes. Place the dough circles on greased baking sheets.
3. Coat them with olive oil. Top them with garlic and tomato, basterma and saguk followed by mozzarella and kaskaval cheese.
4. Season them with some salt and pepper. Pour some olive oil all over them. Place the pizzas in the oven and cook them for 9 to 12 min or until they are done.
5. Serve your pizzas warm.
6. Enjoy.

EGYPTIAN
Beef Patties with White Sauce

Prep Time: 2 hr
Total Time: 2 hr 40 mins

Servings per Recipe: 1
Calories   215.1
Fat   16.1g
Cholesterol   34.6mg
Sodium   203.2mg
Carbohydrates   11.2g
Protein   6.5g

Ingredients

Meat:
2 tbsp olive oil
1 small white onion, chopped
4 small garlic cloves, finely chopped
1 lb lean ground sirloin
1 small green bell pepper, finely chopped
2 tbsp chopped hot green chili peppers
1 tsp salt
1 tbsp fresh ground black pepper
1/4 tsp ground cumin
1/4 tsp ground coriander
1/2 tsp freshly grated nutmeg
1/8 tsp ground cardamom
1/2 tsp spanish sweet paprika
Pastry:
20 sheets phyllo dough
12 tbsp unsalted butter, melted
YOGURT SAUCE
1 quart yogurt
2 garlic cloves, finely chopped
1/2 C. extra virgin olive oil
salt

Directions

1. Grease a casserole dish with some butter. Place it aside.
2. To make the filling:
3. Place a large skillet over medium heat. Heat the oil in it. Sauté in it the onion for 6 min. Add the garlic and cook them for 30 sec.
4. Add the beef to the pan. Brown it for 12 min. Add the bell pepper with spices. Cook them for 6 min while breaking the meat. Transfer the mix to a mixing bowl and place it aside.
5. Place a phyllo sheet in the greased casserole dish. Brush it with some melted butter. cover it with another phyllo sheet to make 10 of them in total.
6. Top them with the meat mix. Cover them with a phyllo sheet and brush it with butter. Repeat the process to make another 10 layers in total.
7. To make the sauce:
8. Cover a fine mesh strainer with a piece of cheesecloth. Pour in it the yogurt and cover it with a plastic wrap. Place it in the fridge for an overnight.
9. Get a food processor: Combine in it the strained yogurt with garlic and process them for 40 sec. Add the oil in a steady stream while processing them all the time.
10. Transfer the sauce mix to a bowl. Add a pinch of salt and stir it well. Place it in the fridge until ready to serve.
11. Spread some melted butter over the top of the pie and cook it in the oven for 42 min. Serve it warm with the yogurt sauce.
12. Enjoy.

Egyptian
Masa'a
(Roasted Vegetable Pan)

Prep Time: 15 mins
Total Time: 1 hr 45 mins

Servings per Recipe: 8
Calories   355.8
Fat   6.0g
Cholesterol   0.0mg
Sodium   0.0mg
Carbohydrates   848.0mg
Protein   68.2g

Ingredients

2 tbsp canola oil
4 tsp minced garlic
1 large onion
4 tsp ground cumin
4 tsp ground coriander
1 eggplant
2 zucchini
1 pattypan squash
1 red pepper
2 large potatoes
2 (19 oz) cans chickpeas
2 (28 oz) cans diced tomatoes

Directions

1. Before you do anything preheat the oven to 325 F. Slice the veggies into 1 inch pieces.
2. Place a pan over medium heat. Heat the oil in it. Sauté in it the garlic with onion and spices. Cook them for 4 min.
3. Stir in the veggies then season them with some salt and pepper. Transfer the mix to a greased casserole dish. Cook it in the oven for 1 h 35 min. Serve it warm.
4. Enjoy.

EGYPTIAN
Molokheya

Prep Time: 4 mins
Total Time: 14 mins

Servings per Recipe: 2
Calories   73.1
Fat   6.7g
Cholesterol   15.2mg
Sodium   1216.0mg
Carbohydrates   4.3g
Protein   0.9g

Ingredients

14 oz frozen molukhia
1 tbsp butter
1 tbsp garlic, minced
1 tsp salt
2 tbsp ground coriander

Directions

1. Place a large skillet over medium heat. Melt the butter in it. Add the molukhia and cook it for 3 min.
2. Stir in the garlic with coriander and a pinch of salt. Sauté them for 4 min. Serve it warm with some flat bread.
3. Enjoy.

Egyptian Shakshuka (Poached Eggs)

Prep Time: 10 mins
Total Time: 30 mins

Servings per Recipe: 3
Calories   251.6
Fat   10.3g
Cholesterol   423.0mg
Sodium   546.8mg
Carbohydrates   24.3g
Protein   15.3g

Ingredients

- olive oil
- 1 onion, chopped
- 3 large garlic, minced
- salt and pepper
- 1 pinch allspice
- 1/4 C. Italian parsley, finely chopped
- 1 (8 oz) cans tomato sauce
- 16 oz water
- 1/4 C. rice
- 6 eggs

Directions

1. Place a large skillet over medium heat. Coat it with olive oil and heat it. Sauté in it the onion, garlic and salt, pepper, and allspice for 4 min.
2. Add the parsley and cook them for 4 min. Make 6 wells in the pan and break an egg in each one. Season them with some salt and pepper.
3. Put on the lid and cook them for 3 to 5 min or until the eggs are done. Serve it warm.
4. Enjoy.

EGYPTIAN
Fish Kabobs

⊛ Prep Time: 10 mins
⏱ Total Time: 25 mins

Servings per Recipe: 6
Calories   390.9
Fat   20.9 g
Cholesterol   46.4 mg
Sodium   474.7 mg
Carbohydrates   28.2 g
Protein   24.1 g

Ingredients

1 1/2 lbs cubed sea bass
16 mushroom caps
2 green peppers, cut in chunks
1/4 C. vinegar
1 tsp salt
1/4 tsp pepper
16 oz chunk pineapple

3 onions, cut in chunks
3 tomatoes, firm, cut in wedges
1/2 C. oil
1 dash cayenne
1/4 tsp mustard powder

Directions

1. Get a large mixing bowl: Whisk in it the vinegar, salt and pepper. Add the fish and stir it for 1 h 30 min.
2. Drain the fish dices and thread them into skewers, with mushroom, peppers, pineapple chunks, onions with tomato while alternating between them. Brush the kebobs with the marinade.
3. Preheat the grill and grease its grates. Cook in it the skewers for 6 to 10 min or until they are done.
4. Enjoy.

Chicken Soup Arabiya

Prep Time: 20 mins
Total Time: 1 hr 50 mins

Servings per Recipe: 4
Calories   831.9
Fat   49.3g
Cholesterol   207.1mg
Sodium   764.7mg
Carbohydrates   39.9g
Protein   56.2g

Ingredients

8 C. water
2 cardamom pods
1 (2 1/2 lb) whole chickens, skinned
1 large onion, halved
1 bay leaf
2 (10 oz) packages fresh spinach
1 tbsp olive oil

2 tsp ground coriander
3/4 tsp salt
10 garlic cloves, crushed
3 tbsp fresh lemon juice
2 C. hot cooked rice

Directions

1. Place a large stock pot over medium heat. Stir in it the water, cardamom pods, chicken, onion and bay leaves. Cook them until they start boiling.
2. Lower the heat and cook them for 1 h 10 min. Turn off the heat. Drain the chicken and place it aside to lose heat.
3. Pour the chicken liquid in a fine mesh sieve and strain it. Reserve the broth with onion. Discard the rest of the strained ingredients.
4. Pour the broth back into the pot. Shred the chicken and stir it back into the pot.
5. Press the strained onion from the broth with a fork. Stir into the pot. Cook them until they start boiling. Stir in the spinach and cook the soup for 6 to 8 min.
6. Place a large pan over medium heat. Heat the oil in it. Sauté in it the garlic with coriander and a pinch of salt. Cook them for half a minute.
7. Stir the garlic mix to the stew pot with lemon juice. Adjust the seasoning of the stew then serve it warm.
8. Enjoy.

HOW TO MAKE
Falafels

🥣 Prep Time: 30 mins
🕐 Total Time: 40 mins

Servings per Recipe: 6
Calories 664.3
Fat 23.7g
Cholesterol 0.0mg
Sodium 1612.0mg
Carbohydrates 91.6g
Protein 24.0g

Ingredients

2 C. dried fava beans
1 medium onion, chopped
1 large potato, peeled and quartered
6 garlic cloves
1 tsp ground coriander
1 tsp ground cumin
2 tsp salt
1/2 tsp black pepper
1/2 tsp cayenne pepper
1/2 C. vegetable oil
3 large green onions, chopped small
3/4 C. dried breadcrumbs
1/2 C. deep fried dried onions
1/2 tsp baking soda
1/4 C. sesame seeds, lightly roasted
4 large radishes, sliced
1/2 C. finely chopped fresh parsley
1 large tomatoes, diced
1 large dill pickle, diced
1 medium jalapeno pepper, seeded and diced
6 whole 6 1/2 inch pita bread
1 C. finely shredded lettuce
1/2 tsp beau monde seasoning

Directions

1. Place a large saucepan medium heat. Add the bean and cover it with water. Cook it until it starts boiling. Put on the lid and cook them for 4 min.
2. Turn off the heat and let soak for an overnight. Strain it.
3. Place a small saucepan over medium heat. Place in it the potato and cover it with water. Cook it until becomes soft. Strain it.
4. Get a food processor: Combine in it the beans with potato, onion and garlic. Process them until they become smooth.
5. Combine in the coriander, cumin, salt, black pepper and cayenne pepper. Blend them smooth. Pour the mix into a large mixing bowl.
6. Stir in the green onions, bread crumbs, deep fried dried onions, and baking soda. Stir them well. Shape the mix into small patties. Dust them with some flour followed by sesame seeds.
7. Place a large skillet over medium heat. Heat the oil in it. Cook in it the falafels for 3 min on each side.
8. Get a mixing bowl: Stir in it the radishes, chopped fresh parsley, diced tomato, and diced dill pickle and diced jalapeno pepper. Stir them well to make the salad.
9. Cover pita bread with a paper towel then microwave it for 35 sec over high. Repeat the process with the rest of the pita bread.
10. Place 3 to 4 patties into each pita bread loaf. Top them with 3 tbsp of the salad mix, lettuce, Beau Monde seasoning. Serve them right away.
11. Enjoy.

Cairo Street
Grilled Chicken

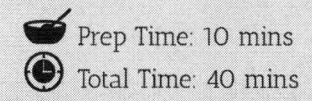

Prep Time: 10 mins
Total Time: 40 mins

Servings per Recipe: 4
Calories	639.1
Fat	57.4g
Cholesterol	80.0mg
Sodium	147.3mg
Carbohydrates	5.5g
Protein	26.9g

Ingredients

500 g chicken breast fillets
4 garlic cloves, crushed
1 C. olive oil
1 C. fresh lemon juice
1/2 tsp lemon zest
2 tsp dried oregano
salt and black pepper

Directions

1. Pat the chicken fillets with some paper towels. Place them aside.
2. Get a small bowl: Mix in it the rest of the ingredients to make the marinade. Stir into the chicken fillets. Pace a piece of wrap over the bowl and place it in the fridge for an overnight.
3. Allow the chicken to rest for 16 min. Drain it from the marinade. Reserve the marinade.
4. Before you do anything preheat grill and grease its grates.
5. Grill in it the chicken fillets for 13 to 15 min on each side while basting them with the marinade every once in a while. Serve it warm.
6. Enjoy.

5-INGREDIENT
Egyptian Rice

Prep Time: 5 mins
Total Time: 30 mins

Servings per Recipe: 4
Calories   366.0
Fat   0.6g
Cholesterol   0.0mg
Sodium   7.8mg
Carbohydrates   80.8g
Protein   6.8g

Ingredients

2 C. rice
oil
1 large onion, diced
3 C. water
salt

Directions

1. Place a large pan over medium heat. Heat the oil in it. Add the onion and cook it for 5 min.
2. Stir in the rice with water and a pinch of salt. Cook it until it starts boiling. Lower the heat and cook the rice until it is done. Serve it warm with some rice.
3. Enjoy.

Egyptian Mashed Carrots

Prep Time: 15 mins
Total Time: 35 mins

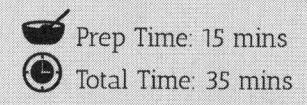

Servings per Recipe: 8
Calories 207.3
Fat 16.3g
Cholesterol 0.0mg
Sodium 85.0mg
Carbohydrates 15.1g
Protein 3.2g

Ingredients

- 1/4 C. blanched almonds or 1/4 C. hazelnuts
- 1/4 C. coriander seed
- 2 tbsp cumin seeds
- 2 tbsp sesame seeds
- 1/4 C. unsweetened dried shredded coconut
- salt
- fresh ground pepper
- 2 lbs carrots, cut into 2-inch lengths
- 6 tbsp extra virgin olive oil, plus more for serving
- 2 tbsp white wine vinegar
- 4 tsp harissa
- 1 tsp ground cumin
- 1/2 tsp ground ginger
- torn pita bread or thinly sliced baguette, for serving

Directions

1. Place a small over medium heat. Toast in it the almonds for 5 min. Place it aside and chop them.
2. Add the cumin seeds with coriander. Cook them for 1 min. Transfer the mix to a mortar or grinder and grind them until they become coarse.
3. Get a mixing bowl: Toss the in it ground spices with chopped almonds. Place it aside.
4. Toast the sesame seeds in the same pan for 1 min. Transfer it to a mortar or grinder. Repeat the process with coconut. Grind them until they become coarse.
5. Stir the coconut and sesame seeds into the almonds mix with 1/2 tsp of salt and pepper.
6. Place a large saucepan over medium heat. Place in it the carrots and cover them with water. Cook them until they start boiling. Lower the heat and cook the carrot for 22 min.
7. Remove them from the water. Discard the water. Cook the carrot in the saucepan for half a minute to dry them.
8. Get a mixing bowl: Chop the carrots and press them with a fork to mash them. Add 6 tbsp of olive oil, the vinegar, harissa, ground cumin and ginger, salt and pepper. Mix them well.
9. Spoon the carrot cream to a serving bowl and top it with the almond mix. Serve it with some pita bread.
10. Enjoy.

EGYPTIAN STUFFED
Mushroom

Prep Time: 20 mins
Total Time: 37 mins

Servings per Recipe: 4
Calories   398.6
Fat   17.5g
Cholesterol   66.0mg
Sodium   362.4mg
Carbohydrates   22.5g
Protein   28.6g

Ingredients

12 fresh large mushrooms, washed and stems removed
2 cloves garlic, finely chopped
2/3 C. plain breadcrumbs
1/4 C. grated parmesan cheese
2 tbsp grated romano cheese
2 tbsp olive oil

2 fluid oz white wine
1 tsp chopped parsley
2 (6 oz) cans minced clams, including juice
1/8 tsp pepper
2 tbsp unsalted butter

Directions

1. Before you do anything preheat the oven to 400 F.
2. Chop about 1 C. of mushroom stems and discard the rest.
3. Get a large mixing bowl: Combine in it the mushroom stems with the rest of the ingredients except for the butter and mushroom caps. Mix them well to make the stuffing.
4. Spoon the stuffing into the mushroom caps and place them on a greased baking sheet. Cook them in the oven for 16 min.
5. Place dollops of butter over the mushroom caps and broil them in the oven for 3 min. Serve them warm.
6. Enjoy.

How to Make
Fava Beans (Fool II)

🥣 Prep Time: 5 mins
🕐 Total Time: 15 mins

Servings per Recipe: 2
Calories   469.3
Fat   22.2g
Cholesterol   0.0mg
Sodium   305.8mg
Carbohydrates   52.8g
Protein   18.0g

Ingredients

1 (16 oz) cans fava beans
3 tbsp canola oil
1/2 tsp cayenne pepper
1/4 tsp salt
1 tsp ground cumin
1 onion
pita bread

Directions

1. Place a pan over medium heat. Heat a splash of oil in it. Finely chop a small onion and sauté it for 3 min.
2. Place a large saucepan over medium heat. Pour the canned beans with its liquid in it. Mash it slightly with a fork or masher. Stir in the lemon juice, salt, ground cumin and cayenne pepper.
3. Stir in a splash of olive oil and cook them until they start boiling. Serve your fava beans with some extra oil on top and your favorite toppings.
4. Enjoy.

EGYPTIAN
Chocolate Cake

🥣 Prep Time: 30 mins
🕐 Total Time: 1 hr 40 mins

Servings per Recipe: 8
Calories 438.0
Fat 15.0g
Cholesterol 138.3mg
Sodium 476.0mg
Carbohydrates 69.5g
Protein 7.1g

Ingredients

1/2 C. powdered chocolate milk mix
4 large eggs, separated
1/2 C. milk
1/2 C. butter
1 1/2 C. sugar
1 3/4 - 2 C. flour, sifted with the salt
1 tsp baking powder

1 tsp salt

Directions

1. Before you do anything preheat the oven to 325 F.
2. Get a small mixing bowl: Stir in it 5 tbsp hot Water with the chocolate milk mix until it is well combined.
3. Get a large mixing bowl: Beat in it the sugar with butter until they become smooth and creamy. Combine the egg yolks and mix them well.
4. Combine in the milk with chocolate mix. Beat them until they become smooth.
5. Combine in the flour and beat them smooth again.
6. Get a mixing bowl: Place in it the egg whites and beat them until their soft peaks. Fold it into the cake batter. Combine in the baking powder with vanilla. Stir them well.
7. Grease a baking pan with some butter and coat it with some flour. Pour the batter cake in it. Cook the cake in the oven for 1 h 12 min.
8. Allow the cake to cool down completely. Serve your cake with your favorite frosting then serve it.
9. Enjoy.

Egyptian Onion and Cucumber Salad

🥣 Prep Time: 1 hr
🕐 Total Time: 1 hr

Servings per Recipe: 4
Calories   380.8
Fat   32.7g
Cholesterol   80.2mg
Sodium   1008.6mg
Carbohydrates   9.7g
Protein   13.5g

Ingredients

1 large English cucumber, peeled, halved lengthwise
salt
12 oz feta cheese
1/2 C. finely chopped walla-walla onion
1/4 C. fresh lemon juice
1/4 C. olive oil
fresh ground pepper
2 tbsp fresh mint sprigs

Directions

1. Pierce the cucumber several times with a fork. Season it with some salt and place it aside for 22 min.
2. Get a serving bowl: Mash the cheese slightly with your hand. Add the onion, lemon juice and oil, a pinch of salt and pepper. Mix them well with a fork.
3. Rinse the cucumber with some cool water. Pat it dry and slice it. Add it to the cheese mix and stir them.
4. Chill the salad in the fridge for 32 min then serve it.
5. Enjoy.

EGYPTIAN
Mihallabiya (Milk Pudding)

Prep Time: 3 mins
Total Time: 11 mins

Servings per Recipe: 4
Calories   205.4
Fat   8.9g
Cholesterol   25.6mg
Sodium   117.8mg
Carbohydrates   24.7g
Protein   7.3g

Ingredients

3 tbsp finely ground rice
3 C. milk
2 1/2 tbsp sugar
1 tbsp rose water
2 tbsp mixed nuts, chopped

Directions

1. Get a mixing bowl: Stir in it 1 C. of milk with rice.
2. Place a large saucepan over medium heat: Combine in it the milk with sugar. Cook them until they start boiling. Add the rice and milk mix. Stir them.
3. Reduce the heat and cook the pudding until it becomes thick. Turn off the heat and add the rosewater. Serve your pudding with some nuts.
4. Enjoy.

Egyptian Eggah (Parsley Omelet)

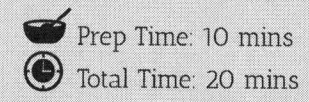

Prep Time: 10 mins
Total Time: 20 mins

Servings per Recipe: 4
Calories   292.3
Fat   24.6g
Cholesterol   317.2mg
Sodium   108.8mg
Carbohydrates   7.8g
Protein   10.4g

Ingredients

- 6 eggs
- 1 tbsp flour
- salt & pepper
- 1 large onion, diced
- 5 tbsp oil
- 1/2 bunch parsley, chopped semi fine
- 1 tomatoes, diced
- 1/2 green bell pepper, diced

Directions

1. Before you do anything preheat the oven broiler.
2. Get a mixing bowl: Whisk in it the eggs with pepper, flour, a pinch of salt and pepper.
3. Place a large skillet over medium heat. Heat 2 tbsp of oil in it. Add the onion and cook it for 3 min.
4. Stir in the tomato with parsley, and pepper for 4 min. Turn off the heat and let them lose heat. Add the beaten eggs and stir them well.
5. Coat an ovenproof pan with the rest of the oil. Place it over medium heat and heat it. Spread the eggs and veggies mix in it.
6. Cook it for 3 to 5 min or until the omelet is set on the bottom. Transfer the pan to the oven and broil it for 4 min. Serve it warm.
7. Enjoy.

EGYPTIAN
Stuffed Grape Leaves (Dolmas)

🥣 Prep Time: 1 hr
🕐 Total Time: 1 hr

Servings per Recipe: 20
Calories   111.5
Fat   7.0g
Cholesterol   20.1mg
Sodium   135.8mg
Carbohydrates   6.0g
Protein   5.4g

Ingredients

1 1/4 lbs ground beef
3/4 C. long grain rice, cooked
1 small onion, chopped fine
2 garlic cloves, crushed or minced)
1 tsp salt
1/4 tsp black pepper
1/4 tsp ground cumin

1 (1 quart) jar pickled grape leaves, in brine, well rinsed and drained, stems cut off
2 tbsp olive oil
1 tbsp lemon juice

Directions

1. Get a large mixing bowl: Combine in it the beef with rice, onion, garlic, cumin, salt and pepper. Mix them well.
2. Shape some of mix into strip like your index finger. Place a grape leaf over a working surface. Place the stuffing log in the middle of the leaf.
3. Lay the bottom and upper sides over the filling and roll it. Place it in a greased casserole dish. Repeat the process with the rest of the ingredients.
4. Lay the stuffed leaves in a greased casserole pan without leaving any emptiness between them. Pour enough water to cover the stuffed leaves.
5. Drizzle the lemon juice with olive oil and stir them gently. Place it over high medium heat. Cook it until it starts boiling. Lower the heat and cook it for 22 min.
6. Serve your stuffed leaves warm.
7. Enjoy.

Egyptian Koras (Vanilla Bread)

Prep Time: 3 hr
Total Time: 3 hr 10 mins

Servings per Recipe: 1
Calories   260.6
Fat   11.3g
Cholesterol   29.1mg
Sodium   20.0mg
Carbohydrates   34.0g
Protein   5.5g

Ingredients

- 1 kg all-purpose flour
- 1 C. ghee or 1 C. butter
- 1/2 C. cream
- 1 pinch salt
- 1/2 tsp vanilla
- 2 tbsp instant yeast
- 3 -4 tbsp sugar
- 1/2 liter sour milk or 1/2 liter yogurt
- 1 tbsp anise
- 1 tbsp fennel seed
- 1 tbsp sesame seeds

Directions

1. Get a large mixing bowl: Combine in it the four with sugar, seeds, yeast, vanilla and salt. Mix them well.
2. Place a small saucepan over medium heat. Melt the butter in it. Transfer it to the flour mix. Mix them well.
3. Combine in the yogurt with cream. Mix them well with your hands until your get a smooth dough. Place a kitchen towel over the dough and let it rise for 30 min.
4. Divide the dough into several egg sized pieces. Cover them with a kitchen towel and let them rise for 2 h 10 min.
5. Place a piece of dough in a floured working surface. Roll it in the shape of circle with you hands. Repeat the process with the rest of the dough.
6. Place the dough circles on greased baking sheets and let them rest for 1 h.
7. Before you do anything preheat the oven to 356 F.
8. Get a small mixing bowl: Whisk in it some milk with vanilla and an egg. Make several parallel lines with a knife on top of the bread circles.
9. Brush them with the vanilla mix. Cook them in them for 16 min. Serve your bread warm with some sweet or savory toppings.
10. Enjoy.

ALEXANDRIA
Chocolate Cake

Prep Time: 30 mins
Total Time: 1 hr 30 mins

Servings per Recipe: 12
Calories   551.6
Fat   18.4g
Cholesterol   126.7mg
Sodium   453.0mg
Carbohydrates   90.3g
Protein   7.9g

Ingredients

3 C. all-purpose flour
2 1/2 C. granulated sugar
3/4 C. brown sugar
1 tbsp pumpkin pie spice or 1 tbsp apple pie spice
1 1/2 tsp baking powder
1 1/2 tsp baking soda
1/2 tsp salt
6 oz milk chocolate chips
1 (15 oz) cans pumpkin
3/4 C. melted butter or 3/4 C. margarine
6 eggs, slightly beaten or 6 equivalent egg substitute

Directions

1. Before you do anything preheat the oven to 350 F. Grease a loaf pan.
2. Get a mixing bowl: Combine in it pumpkin, melted butter and eggs. Mix them well.
3. Get a large mixing bowl: Mix in it the flour with white and brown sugar, baking powder and soda, salt. Add the pumpkin mix. Whisk them well. Fold in the chocolate chips.
4. Pour the batter into the load pan. Cook it in the oven for 1 h 5 min. Allow the cake to cool down completely then serve it.
5. Enjoy.

Ful Mudammes (Fava Bean Spread)

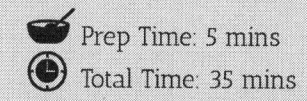

Prep Time: 5 mins
Total Time: 35 mins

Servings per Recipe: 4
Calories   139.4
Fat   0.7g
Cholesterol   0.0mg
Sodium   14.9mg
Carbohydrates   25.8g
Protein   8.9g

Ingredients

- 1 (15 oz) cans cooked fava beans or 1 1/2 C. cooked fava beans
- 1 small onion, chopped
- 3 garlic cloves, chopped
- 1 large tomatoes, chopped
- 1/2 tsp chili powder
- 1/2 tsp curry powder
- 1/2 tsp cumin
- 1 dash cinnamon
- 1 dash clove
- 1 dash turmeric
- 1 dash cayenne
- 1 tbsp lemon juice
- salt
- 1 small potato, peeled and cooked, added when onion is cooking (optional)

Directions

1. Place a large pan over medium heat. Heat a splash of oil in it. Sauté in it the onion for 3 min. Stir in the garlic and cook them for 1 min.
2. Stir in the tomato and cook them for 4 min until it softens. Stir in the lemon juice with spices, a pinch of salt and pepper.
3. Cook them for 18 min over low heat while stirring them occasionally. Serve it with some extra olive oil.
4. Enjoy.

OMM 'ALI
(Bread Pudding)

🥣 Prep Time: 20 mins
🕒 Total Time: 50 mins

Servings per Recipe: 4
Calories 281.6
Fat 24.0g
Cholesterol 16.1mg
Sodium 260.1mg
Carbohydrates 12.0g
Protein 8.1g

Ingredients

1 packet roqaq (Bread crackers)
1 C. mixed nuts
1 tbsp coconut, grated
1 tbsp unsalted butter or 1 tbsp fresh cream
1 C. milk, sweetened

Directions

1. Before you do anything preheat the oven to 365 F. Grease a casserole dish.
2. Place 2 sheets of the roqaq on a baking sheet and dry them in the oven for 3 min until they become crispy. Repeat the process with the rest of the crackers.
3. Press the crackers with your hands. Lay it in the greased dish then top it with the nuts and coconut.
4. Place a small saucepan over medium heat. Heat the milk in it. Drizzle it all over the pudding mix then dot it with butter.
5. Cook in it the oven until it becomes golden brown on top. Serve it warm.
6. Enjoy.

Egyptian Lentil Hot Pot

Prep Time: 5 mins
Total Time: 35 mins

Servings per Recipe: 6
Calories   214.5
Fat   8.3g
Cholesterol   20.3mg
Sodium   75.1mg
Carbohydrates   26.7g
Protein   9.5g

Ingredients

- 5 C. vegetable stock
- 1 C. brown lentils, washed and drained
- 2 large onions, chopped
- 2 medium tomatoes, finely chopped
- 4 garlic cloves, crushed
- 4 tbsp butter
- 2 tsp cumin
- 1 pinch salt and pepper, to taste
- 4 tsp lemon juice

Directions

1. Place a large saucepan over medium heat. Pour in it the stock and cook it until it starts boiling. Stir in the lentils and 2/3 of the onions, tomatoes, and garlic.
2. Cook them until they start boiling again. Lower the heat and cook them for 15 to 25 min until the lentils are done.
3. Place a large skillet over medium heat. Place in it the butter and heat it until it melts. Add the rest of the onion and cook it for 4 min.
4. Get a food processor: Allow the soup to cool down slightly then blend it smooth in batches. Pour the soup back into the saucepan.
5. Cook the soup for 5 min. Add the cumin, salt, pepper, lemon juice and remaining 2 tbsp of butter. Serve your soup hot and top it with the sautéed onion.
6. Enjoy.

BANGAR BIL ZABADI
(Classical Beet Salad)

Prep Time: 10 mins
Total Time: 1 hr 10 mins

Servings per Recipe: 4
Calories 71.7
Fat 2.1g
Cholesterol 7.9mg
Sodium 73.8mg
Carbohydrates 10.6g
Protein 3.5g

Ingredients

1/2 lb beet, boiled and diced
3 1/2 oz tomatoes, diced
3 1/2 oz cucumbers, diced
1 C. yoghurt
1 garlic clove, minced
salt, to taste

Directions

1. Get a small mixing bowl: Whisk in it the yogurt with garlic and a pinch of salt to make the dressing.
2. Get a serving bowl: Toss in it the veggies with the yogurt dressing. Place it in the fridge for 1 h 10 min. Serve it.
3. Enjoy.

Fahmi's Zucchini (Kosa Matbukha Bi l Zabadi)

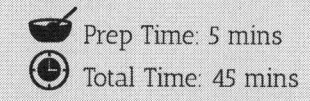

Prep Time: 5 mins
Total Time: 45 mins

Servings per Recipe: 8
Calories   88.3
Fat   5.6g
Cholesterol   7.3mg
Sodium   42.6mg
Carbohydrates   6.7g
Protein   3.8g

Ingredients

2 lbs zucchini, medium sized
1 lb yoghurt
1 egg white
salt, to taste
1 tsp cornstarch
1/2 C. mint leaf, chopped
2 tbsp olive oil

Directions

1. Before you do anything preheat the oven to 350 F.
2. Get a small mixing bowl: Whisk in it the yoghurt, egg white, cornstarch and salt.
3. Place a large saucepan over medium heat. Heat the oil in it. Cut the zucchini into slices and cook them until they become golden brown on both sides.
4. Lay the zucchini slices in a greased casserole dish. Spread the yogurt mix over it. Cook it in the oven for 18 min.
5. Top it with the mint leaves. Cook it in the oven for 6 min then serve it warm.
6. Enjoy.

ALTERNATIVE
Koshari

🥣 Prep Time: 15 mins
🕐 Total Time: 30 mins

Servings per Recipe: 8
Calories   231.9
Fat   1.0g
Cholesterol   0.0mg
Sodium   269.7mg
Carbohydrates   50.4g
Protein   6.9g

Ingredients

- 2 C. cooked rice
- 2 C. cooked penne pasta
- 2 tbsp white vinegar
- 1 tsp ground cumin, divided
- 1/2 tsp garlic powder
- 1 C. cooked lentils
- 1 (15 oz) cans crushed tomatoes
- 1/2 C. water
- 1 1/2 tbsp sugar
- 3/4 tsp ground cinnamon
- 1/2 tsp salt
- 1/4 tsp crushed red pepper flakes
- 3 medium yellow squash, cut into 1/2-inch pieces
- 2 medium onions, thinly sliced

Directions

1. Get a large mixing bowl: Whisk in it the vinegar, 1/2 tsp cumin, and garlic powder. Stir in the lentils.
2. Place a saucepan over medium heat: Cook in it the tomatoes, water, sugar, cinnamon, salt, remaining 1/2 tsp cumin and red pepper for 6 min. Fold in the squash.
3. Divide the warm rice over serving plates then top them with warm pasta, lentils and tomato sauce. Serve your Koshari warm.
4. Enjoy.

Dukka (Egyptian Spice Blend)

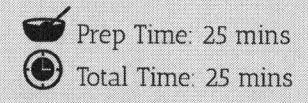

Prep Time: 25 mins
Total Time: 25 mins

Servings per Recipe: 1
Calories   1471.8
Fat   124.9g
Cholesterol   0.0mg
Sodium   2407.0mg
Carbohydrates   86.7g
Protein   45.3g

Ingredients

- 4 oz sesame seeds
- 3 oz hazelnuts or 3 oz roasted chickpeas
- 2 oz coriander seeds
- 1 oz cumin seed
- 1 tsp sea salt
- 1/2 tsp ground black peppercorns
- 1 tsp dried thyme or 1 tsp mint

Directions

1. Place a small pan over medium heat. Toast in it the sesame seeds. Place it aside.
2. Add the hazelnuts and toast them for 6 min. Discard their skin. Place them aside.
3. Add the coriander with cumin seeds and toast them until they become dark in color. Place them aside to lose heat.
4. Get a food processor or coffee grinder. Combine in it all the ingredients and grind them until they become coarse. Store them in a jar for up to 90 days.
5. Enjoy.

EGYPTIAN
Raspberry and Peach Fruit Cups

Prep Time: 5 mins
Total Time: 15 mins

Servings per Recipe: 4
Calories   532.9
Fat   20.5g
Cholesterol   3.6mg
Sodium   698.0mg
Carbohydrates   79.7g
Protein   10.5g

Ingredients

2 C. raspberries
3 tsp caster sugar
2 peaches
4 C. strawberries
8 biscuits

Directions

1. Place a heavy saucepan over medium heat. Stir in it the sugar with raspberries. Bring them to a simmer over low heat. Simmer them for 6 min. Place the mix aside to lose heat.
2. Get a blender: Combine in it the peaches with the raspberries mix. Blend them smooth. Pour the mix in a fine mesh sieve and strain it.
3. Transfer the strained sauce into a mixing bowl. Stir into it the strawberries. Divide the mix between serving glasses.
4. Top them with the ginger biscuits. Chill them in the fridge until ready to serve.
5. Enjoy.

Egyptian Rice Pudding

Prep Time: 2 hr 10 mins
Total Time: 2 hr 20 mins

Servings per Recipe: 6
Calories	325.2
Fat	9.2g
Cholesterol	34.1mg
Sodium	119.5mg
Carbohydrates	52.1g
Protein	9.1g

Ingredients

- 3/4 C. rice flour
- 3/4 C. sugar
- 6 C. milk
- 2 whole green cardamom pods, lightly crushed
- 1 pinch saffron thread
- 3 tbsp rose water
- chopped pistachios, to garnish

Directions

1. Place a heavy saucepan over medium heat. Stir in it the sugar with flour and milk. Cook them until they start boiling while mixing all the time.
2. Stir in the saffron with cardamom. Cook them for 2 min while stirring all the time. Fold in the rosewater.
3. Divide the pudding between serving glasses. Chill them in the fridge for 2 h 30 min. Serve them with your favorite toppings.
4. Enjoy.

CAULIFLOWER
(قرنبيط)

🥣 Prep Time: 10 mins
🕐 Total Time: 30 mins

Servings per Recipe: 4
Calories   284 kcal
Fat   13.4g
Cholesterol   48mg
Sodium   102mg
Carbohydrates   34.2g
Fiber   4.8g
Protein   8.7g

Ingredients

2 tsps ground cumin
1 head cauliflower, cut into florets
1 C. all-purpose flour
1 egg
2 cloves garlic
1 tsp ground cumin

1 tbsp tomato paste
salt to taste
1/4 C. milk, or as needed
2 C. vegetable oil, or as needed

Directions

1. Cook cauliflower florets in boiling salty water for 2 minutes, while adding two tsps of cumin and then a blended mixture of tomato paste, salt, flour, egg, cumin and garlic.
2. Cook everything in hot oil 8 minutes or until golden.
3. Serve.

Feta Omelet (عجة الجبن)

Prep Time: 5 mins
Total Time: 10 mins

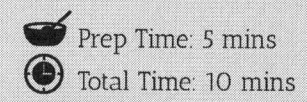

Servings per Recipe: 2
Calories   243 kcal
Fat   19.8g
Cholesterol   385mg
Sodium   300mg
Carbohydrates   1.8g
Fiber   0.1g
Protein   14.7g

Ingredients

4 eggs, beaten
1/2 tsp black pepper
3 tbsp crumbled feta cheese
1 tsp milk
1 tbsp vegetable oil

Directions

1. Cook a mixture of beaten eggs and pepper in hot oil and then add a mixture of milk and cheese when the edges are cooked before folding it up around this cheese mixture.
2. Enjoy.

ENJOY THE RECIPES?

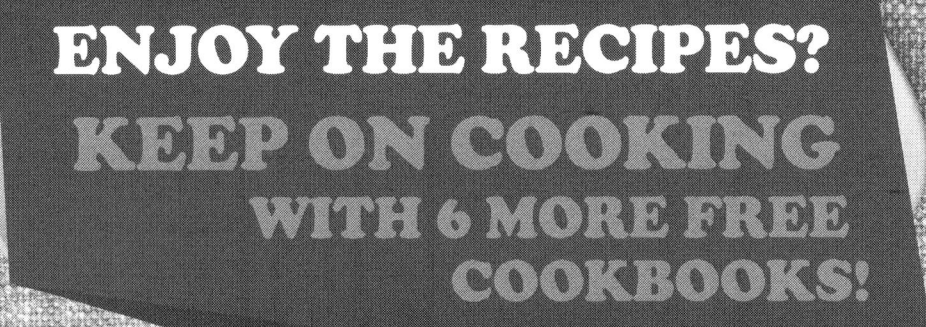

KEEP ON COOKING WITH 6 MORE FREE COOKBOOKS!

Visit our website and simply enter your email address to join the club and receive your 6 cookbooks.

http://booksumo.com/magnet

https://www.instagram.com/booksumopress/

https://www.facebook.com/booksumo/

Manufactured by Amazon.ca
Bolton, ON

42601892R00033